Hist YA 902.07 G197

The Gang of eight
  $17.95

D1479638

MAIN LIBRARY

Memphis and Shelby
County Public Library and
Information Center

For the Residents
of
Memphis and Shelby County

The Gang of Eight

With an Introduction by Tom Brokaw

Tony Auth, *Philadelphia Inquirer*
Paul Conrad, *Los Angeles Times*
Jules Feiffer, *Village Voice*
Jeff MacNelly, *Chicago Tribune*
Doug Marlette, *Charlotte Observer*
Mike Peters, *Dayton Daily News*
Paul Szep, *Boston Globe*
Don Wright, *Miami News*

faber and faber

BOSTON • LONDON

Library of Congress Cataloging in Publication Data
Main entry under title:

The Gang of eight.

1. World politics—1945- —Caricatures and cartoons 2. United States—Politics and
government—1945- —Caricatures and cartoons. 3. American wit and humor, Pictorial.
D844.G33 1985   902′.07   84-28699
ISBN 0-571-12531-X (pbk.)

The Gang of Eight copyright 1985 by Faber & Faber, Inc. All rights reserved. Printed in the United States
of America. No part of this book may be used or reproduced in any manner whatsoever without written
permission. For information write to the publisher, Faber & Faber, Inc., 39 Thompson Street, Winchester,
MA 01890.

Tony Auth's cartoons © by Tony Auth. Reprinted with permission.
Paul Conrad's cartoons © by *The Los Angeles Times*. Reprinted with permission.
Jules Feiffer's cartoons © by Jules Feiffer. Reprinted with permission.
Jeff MacNelly's cartoons © by Jeff MacNelly. Reprinted with permission.
Doug Marlette's cartoons © by Doug Marlette. Reprinted with permission.
Mike Peters' cartoons © by *United Feature Syndicate*. Reprinted with permission.
Paul Szep's cartoons © by *The Boston Globe*. Reprinted with permission.
Don Wright's cartoons © by Don Wright. Reprinted with permission.

ISBN 0 571 12531 X
Library of Congress Catalog Number 84-28699

MEMPHIS/SHELBY COUNTY PUBLIC LIBRARY
AND INFORMATION CENTER

Contents

Introduction

To begin, a small confession: I never met a political cartoonist I didn't like in person or on paper. That sounds like hyperbole but it's true. I've come to know most of America's celebrated political cartoonists, and I'm hard put to find much fault with any of them. So much for objectivity.

That will disappoint a lot of people. After all, sooner or later cartoonists offend just about everyone. "Now this time he's gone too far!" is a standard reaction to any one of the Gang of Eight. It would be a lot easier for the offended, whether they come from the far left, far right or somewhere in between, if these gentlemen had some kind of obvious character or intellectual defect.

As for the cartoonists, it is just as well they are known for their work and not for their personalities. Otherwise the impact of what they have to say through their drawings would be diluted, sort of like converting horseradish to apple pie. Reactions would change from "Now he's goe too far!" to "Yeah, that is outrageous but he's such a nice guy." Indeed, I worry I may have compromised their standing with just these few lines so let us get on with their work.

We live in the age of information. The news cycle runs twenty-four hours a day over the air and in print. The speed and the density of this mass of information is astonishing. If something newsworthy happens it is nearly impossible not to know about it, moving as it does from wire service to all-news radio to all-news television to local television to network television to newspapers to news magazines and, often, back again. It can be exhausting. Within a very short time period a piece of news loses its vitality. It is drained of its capacity to interest and arouse us. We lower our guard.

Then — ZAP! — the political cartoonist strikes. The news lives again. Trappings and obfuscation are stripped away. Behold, a new truth. Yes, a truth, for in these cartoons we find a simple, true vision, one man's reaction to the maniacal, the tragic, the comic, the amazing world in which we live.

Moreover, it is an enduring vision, usually strengthened by the passage of time, as these cartoons will remind you. For example, there is a good deal of talk about the revival of Richard Nixon. Measure that talk against Paul Conrad's Nixon as King Richard or Nixon in Conrad's spider web. Which do you think will be the lasting impression?

Is there any more eloquent statement about the frustration of black America than Jules Feiffer's black man describing whitey's exploitation of black contributions?

For all that has been written and broadcast about the complexities of Lebanon, Tony Auth's Beirut gunfight may be the best summary.

Jeff MacNelly's 1040 tax form reduces the massive U.S. tax code to its essential absurdity. Let the debate over tax reform begin and end with this cartoon.

Even the remaining segregationists must be a little uncomfortable with their hypocrisy when they see Doug Marlette's operator of a white Christian academy struggling with his tax-exempt status.

Mike Peters, a self-described class clown, makes you laugh so hard you want to cry over his cartoon about the mother whose son has grown a foot.

Jimmy Carter's partisans will strive mightily to enhance his standing with future historians, but I doubt they'll be able to overcome Paul Szep's Jimmy Carter as a Boy Scout.

Political cartoonists have a special sensitivity to the strength of a political ideal so it is appropriate that one of them, Don Wright, has eloquently captured the essence of Solidarity: the strength of its ideals.

These contributions from individual members of the Gang of Eight are bound together by a common trait: a fierce independence from the constraints of conventional wisdom and the political establishment. They speak for those who have no voice in the big arena of public affairs. They say, for so many, ''Hey, wait a minute! What in the *world* is going on here?!!?''

For those who are certified members of the power structure, wherever it may exist, the Gang of Eight and their colleagues perform an invaluable service. They give them perspective, often simply by reducing their egos to fit a cartoonist's panel. Can you imagine the pomposity quotient in the political world if there were no political cartoonists?

Moreover, this Gang has honorable antecedents, reaching all the way back to a time when cave men were drawing stick figures on stone walls, interpreting what they had witnessed that day. They trace their honorable calling from those primitive times through Hogarth, Daumier, Goya, Nast.

They marry their artistry to courage and intelligence to bring us insight, laughter and truth. We are richer for their presence.

Tom Brokaw
February 1985

The Gang of Eight

Tony Auth

People often ask "are you fair to the president, to the Catholics, to the power companies" . . . whatever. My first impulse is to say "of course I'm fair," meaning that I'm not an apologist nor a propagandist for some ideology or political party, and that nothing gives me more delight than being happily surprised when someone I've had reason to attack does or says something that I can support. I find though, that more often than not "fairness" is assumed to mean a pro-administration drawing for every one critical of the president, or at least a barb aimed at the Democrats for every one directed at the Republicans (as if the legitimacy of any criticism depended on its being offset, or the credibility of cartoonists could be judged by their ability to leap from side to side). Of course this is ridiculous. Imaging having to do a pro-Hitler cartoon for every one critical of the Nazis.

Our only obligation as artists is to try to tell the truth as we see it. We are offset not by ourselves, but by the works of others—whether they're columnists, editorial writers, other cartoonists, songwriters or film makers whose world view and opinions differ from ours. By the way, I have yet to hear anyone ask George Will why he doesn't do one anti-Reagan column for every one he does critical of Mondale. A point of view evolves over time. It is shaped and honed by experience and surprise, and leads not to faith in a particular dogma, but to more and more deeply felt ideas about the nature and potential of men and women.

One of the things we just have to accept in this work is that we can never be on top of our reading. It's as if we are standing under a waterfall, a torrent of facts, heresay, rumor, lies, distortions, propaganda and half-truths. Trying to sort it all out and comment on it is a never-ending task, and it is our work. I find it refreshing and recreational, in the literal sense of the word, to step back out of that waterfall when it becomes numbing. It is a joy to browse through *The Smithsonian, The National Geographic* or *The New Yorker,* to go to a movie or to spend half an hour with the latest children's book by James Stevenson or William Steig.

I also find it necessary to work at the newspaper, to talk to reporters and editors and to bounce ideas off them. That, by the way, is why we need editors, not to tell us what opinions are acceptable or what to draw, but to tell us when the cartoons don't work. If the guy who is nominally your editor isn't good at this (and many people aren't), you have to find someone who is. I don't know how cartoonists who work at home alone do it. When there's a strike at my newspaper, I continue to work for syndication, but at home. I get up a little later, read a little more slowly, have a third cup of coffee, and before I know it it's two o'clock. I haven't even really begun to work yet. If I'd gone in to the paper I'd be finished.

Finally, a word about ''style.'' Style is the way various cartoonists choose to depict visual information. Since the pictorial content of different drawings has the capacity to arouse very different responses in the reader, it seems natural to approach different drawings in different ways. A whimsical idea should be expressed by a whimsical drawing. A cartoon that is a hearty dismissal of a particular politician or idea is best expressed with a rapid, carefree line. I also experiment a lot. I try new kinds of pens, nibs, brushes and different types of paper. Having said all that, it is nonetheless true that almost anything I did five years ago looks quite strange to me now, as if someone else did it—which, in a way, is true.

"I've gotta stop smoking grass.
It makes me paranoid."

There will be six hours of football on television Christmas Day.

—News Item

'The problem of the ghettos? The ghettos, my dear, are a solution, not a problem.'

Albert Einstein, 1879 — 1955

ANWAR SADAT 1918-1981

SHE ASKED FOR IT.
SHE WORE A TIGHT SWEATER.

HE ASKED FOR IT.
HE BOUGHT A BMW.

THEY ASKED FOR IT. THEY MOVED
INTO A WHITE NEIGHBORHOOD.

HE ASKED FOR IT. HE PUT IN A GOVERNMENT I DON'T LIKE.

'IN THE NAME OF THE FATHER, AND OF THE SON...'

Paul Conrad

What could be more unfair than asking a cartoonist who has been drawing for thirty-three years to name his twenty best cartoons? It's like asking a touring pro to name his twenty best approach shots. He remembers every one of them landing up against the pin.

It's easier to name my most important cartoon. As I've said before, that's the one that will be in the paper tomorrow. It may not be perfect, but it's finished. When you live with pen in hand, swinging between revelation and despair, being finished is important.

Some I chose just because I like them. Some I hope are timeless and will have meaning into the next generation. Some survived bitter criticism the day they were printed and now seem so obviously true.

All made a statement, and that's what political cartooning is all about. An effective cartoon says something, without weaseling, about an issue, a personality, a triumph or a terrible injustice—about war, poverty, peace and those marvelous days when mankind gets a little leg up on the world. The very best cartoons say things that would be difficult and sometimes impossible to put in words.

They have one other important thing in common. None could have been drawn or published without the freedom guaranteed by that granite foundation of democracy, the First Amendment.

1971, The Register
and Tribune Syndicate

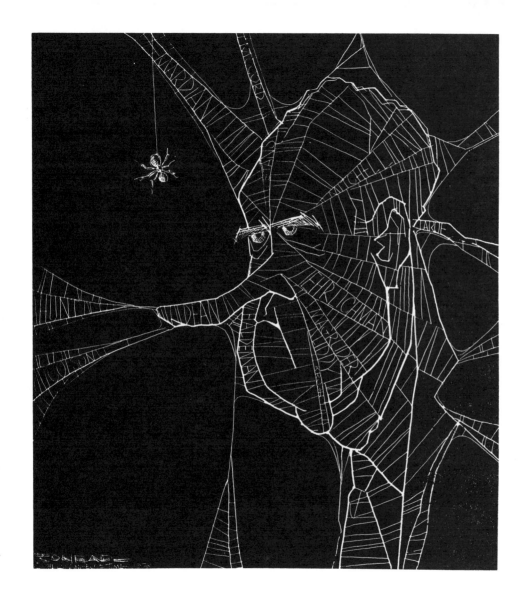

30 The Gang of Eight

O THAT I WERE AS GREAT AS MY GRIEF, OR LESSER THAN MY NAME!
OR THAT I COULD FORGET WHAT I HAVE BEEN!
OR NOT REMEMBER WHAT I MUST BE NOW!
KING RICHARD II. ACT III, SCENE III

WHERE HAVE ALL THE LEADERS GONE?

INDEPENDENCE HALL

© THE LOS ANGELES TIMES, 1977

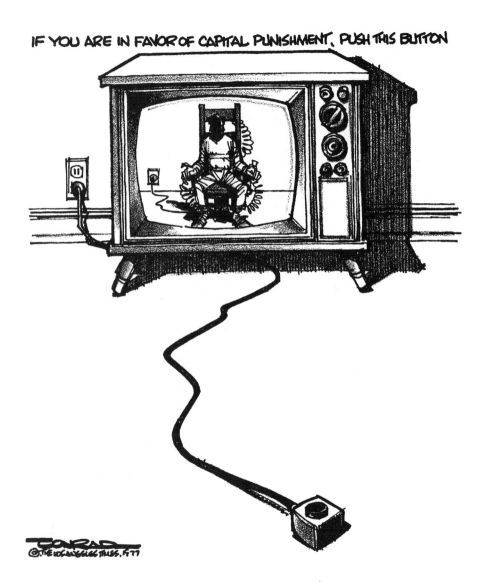

SPEAKING OF AMERICAN CULTS...

THE EIGHTH WONDER OF THE WORLD

CALIFORNIA SYNDROME

MICROSCOPIC VIEW OF BACTERIA DEVELOPED TO EAT OIL

REFLECTIONS ON MRS. REAGAN'S NEW WHITE HOUSE CHINA

"THEN IT'S AGREED... YOU'LL TAKE CARE OF THE POOR
AND I'LL TAKE CARE OF THE RICH!"

Paul Conrad 43

STILL LIFE

Paul Conrad 45

ONE GIANT STEP FOR WOMANKIND

" PLAY IT AGAIN, RON... "

"FOUR MORE YEARS!"

Jules Feiffer

I started drawing at four, loved comic strips, loved comic books (which were different), and wanted more than anything else in life to write and draw a syndicated daily and Sunday page just like the great cartoonists I admired: Caniff, Capp, Crane, Segar. This was the 1930s.

Another early hero was Will Eisner, creator of ''The Spirit,'' a weekly comic book that ran as a Sunday supplement in several dozen newspapers. Eisner gave me my first job in comics when I was sixteen. This was in 1947. He let me erase pages for a year, then another year he let me fill in blacks, then another year he let me rule panel borders. That same year, searching for other work he could trust me with, he let me ghostwrite his scripts. Ghosting ''The Spirit''! I was in cartoonists' heaven.

I was a passive fellow, hard to satisfy but harder to move. Had the army not drafted me in 1951 at the end of the Korean War, I might not have strayed into satire. But the army was my first trip away from home. It taught me mindless labor, alienation, abuse of power and, in general, the coldness of wordly authority when not under the guidance of my mother.

In the army I learned about language as dogma, also language as code and lies. I learned about the loss of innocence, followed by rage, followed by a thirst for vengeance, a need to tell all in public.

I came out of the army a subversive cartoonist. This was a time known as McCarthyism. There was no call for subversive cartoonists.

My satires flowed out of spite: one about a four year old drafted into the army by mistake, one about the biggest bomb in the world, one about a young conformist who became a facsimile of whichever group he was momentarily part of. None sold. Three years went by. I took to stopping editors in the street. It didn't help. *The Village Voice,* a small Greenwich Village weekly, came into being. It agreed to publish my drawings without censorship, without editing and without fee. This was 1956.

Twenty-nine years later, I am still at *The Voice*. And I am paid. And I am syndicated. And I am in *Playboy,* with a series on divorced middle-aged men. And I am a formerly divorced middle-aged man who has remarried. And things out there are as bad, and possibly worse, than when I learned rage in the United States Army and became a subversive.

But it is more than a generation later, and the country feels less threatened by subversives—especially the kind who draw and write. The country has learned that it is too big, blasé, uncoordinated and short of memory to change fast or change much. The country has learned that it appreciates the perks of middle-class privilege too much to pay attention to grousing on the Left. It has forgotten the existence of an American Left, connects it somehow to Mondale and liberalism. The remnant Left continues to picket in peace. No one remembers it. It scarcely remembers itself.

I have a second daughter, born almost twenty-one years after my first. As I write this, she is asleep, some six hours after her last feeding, which was at 3:45 in the morning, two weeks to the minute after she was born. Much of my time from here on will be joining this piece of information with less friendly pieces of information, and out of all of it constructing an attitude and a politics and a life.

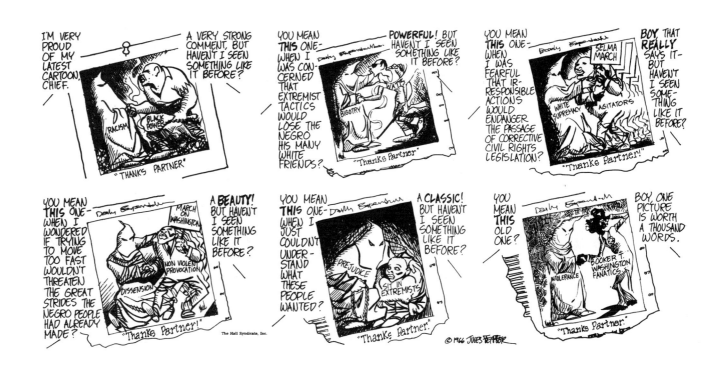

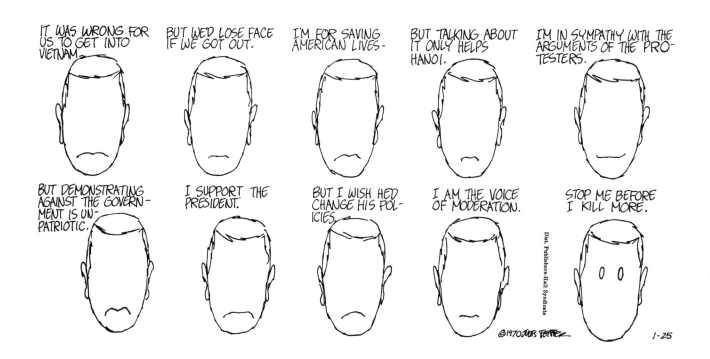

IT WAS WRONG FOR US TO GET INTO VIETNAM.

BUT WE'D LOSE FACE IF WE GOT OUT.

I'M FOR SAVING AMERICAN LIVES—

BUT TALKING ABOUT IT ONLY HELPS HANOI.

I'M IN SYMPATHY WITH THE ARGUMENTS OF THE PROTESTERS.

BUT DEMONSTRATING AGAINST THE GOVERNMENT IS UNPATRIOTIC.

I SUPPORT THE PRESIDENT.

BUT I WISH HE'D CHANGE HIS POLICIES.

I AM THE VOICE OF MODERATION.

STOP ME BEFORE I KILL MORE.

Dist. Publishers-Hall Syndicate

©1970 JULES FEIFFER

1-25

S.D.S. STEALS SECRET PAPERS FROM HARVARD.

HARVARD IS EMBARRASSED BY SENSATIONAL DISCLOSURES.

REVOLUTIONARIES STEAL SECRET PAPERS FROM F.B.I. IN MEDIA, PA.

F.B.I. IS EMBARRASSED BY SENSATIONAL DISCLOSURES.

NEW YORK TIMES OBTAINS SECRET PAPERS FROM GOVERNMENT.

GOVERNMENT IS EMBARRASSED BY SENSATIONAL DISCLOSURES.

IN A COLD WAR SOCIETY IF YOU WANT LIES—

YOU GO TO A PRESS CONFERENCE.

IF YOU WANT THE TRUTH—

YOU STEAL IT.

7-18

© 1971 JULES FEIFFER

56   The Gang of Eight

I STONEWALLED THEM
ON THE WAR.

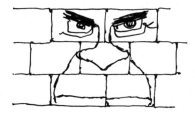

I STONEWALLED THEM
ON THE COVER-UP.

I STONEWALLED THEM ON
THE TAXES.

I STONEWALLED THEM
ON THE TAPES.

I STONEWALLED THEM
ON THE COURTS.

I HAVE NOT YET BEGUN
TO STONEWALL.

REAGAN'S PEOPLE ALWAYS HATED ME.

SINCE HIS ELECTION I FOUND MYSELF LONELY UND UNVANTED...

RESTRICTED TO A TV GHETTO MIT TED KOPPEL UND DAVID HARTMAN UND GEORGE VILL...

TREATING ZESE PEOPLE LIKE EQVALS! COULD YOU BELIEVE IT?

ZEN ZEYMOUR HERSH WRITES A BOOK ACCUSING ME OF BEING A LIAR, A NO-GOOD, PRACTICALLY A VAR CRIMINAL!

RONALD REAGAN SAYS TO HIS PEOPLE, "HEY! VE HAD HENRY ALL WRONG!"

UND ZO I AM BACK DOING VOT I VAS MEANT TO DO...

VORKING FOR THE YANKEE DOLLAH!

DIST UNIVERSAL PRESS SYNDICATE

©1983 Jules Feiffer   8-21

MACNELLY

Jeff MacNelly

Political cartooning is pretty simple—if you have something to say. The drawing is the mechanical part. It's what makes us different from other forms of commentary, but it's only the device we use to express ourselves.

We are always asked who is the easiest or the most fun to draw. They're all easy to draw. Asking a cartoonist that question is like asking a columnist who is the easiest to type out on your VDT. Cartoonists are rarely asked who they like in the majority leader's race and why. Rather, it's always who would you like to see win—from a cartoonist's point of view—i.e., who would be the most fun to draw?

I know, I know, you'd rather see the funny drawings than listen to a cartoonist pontificate, but the point is, a good cartoonist should have a definite point of view, a set of values and opinions. Otherwise, he's just a gag writer.

That's not to say humor in political cartoons is undesirable. Not at all. The basis of effective humor in a political cartoon is ridicule. And ridicule is one of the most powerful and effective nonviolent weapons we humans possess. By subjecting the self-righteous and the pompous to derisive ridicule, we bring them down to earth with the rest of us where we can examine them on our own terms. It's even more fun when these guys have no sense of humor about it all.

Even though our best targets are the self-important and their sacred cows and holy crusades, we cartoonists shouldn't get in the rut of cruising the front page looking for something off of which to launch a laugh. Leave that stuff for Johnny Carson's monologue.

One of the questions we always get is, "Where do you get your ideas?" It is true that most of our topics come from the daily news, and they are easy to find. The difficulty lies in finding the right metaphor to use to express your opinion in the most original and efficient way. That's why I always find it healthy to back away from the piles of daily newspapers once in a while and dive into some opinion magazine or an old *Sports*

Illustrated—or, in my case, often a *Popular Mechanics*—or some book off the shelf. It helps me get away from the constant avalanche of breaking news and information and get a feel for what might really be on people's mind that week or that month.

What also helps me in coming up with my political cartoons is participating in the daily editorial board meeting. I never get any specific direction from anybody on what to draw, but I do find this exercise valuable for two reasons: first, my office is way up on the top of the Tribune Tower. It takes three separate elevator rides for me to reach the newsroom and its nest of editors (a great advantage, by the way). So the morning meeting allows me to kick around thoughts with someone other than the gargoyles that hang around up here in the flying buttresses. Secondly, the editorial meeting is where I get almost all my ideas for my comic strip, *Shoe*.

One last word about my technique or "style." Kids who want to be cartoonists always ask me how I developed my style. I'm still working on it. I usually use brush and ink, but then I discover a handful of neat pen nibs, and I scratch around with them for a while. I am forever messing around with different sizes, types of paper, brushes, pens, inks—everything. So my style is always changing or moving, hopefully evolving. You should never resist the urge to change any aspect of what you do, just because you've discovered a gimmick or a stylistic device that comes easy to you. It's that kind of laziness that keeps cartooning from being recognized as an art form.

'I KNOW WHAT YOU'RE PROBABLY THINKING...'

' WELL, THERE I WAS, PLAYING "HAIL TO THE CHIEF" ON WHAT I <u>THOUGHT</u> WAS MY ACCORDION...'

Jeff MacNelly 85

Form **1040**

US Department of the Treasury - INTERNAL REVENUE SERVICE

US Individual Income Tax Return

1976

FOR THE YEAR JANUARY 1 — DECEMBER 31, 1976, OR WHENEVER YOU GET AROUND TO IT

Please Type or Print

Name **JEFF MACNELLY**

Last Name **MACNELLY**   Second to Last Initial   STARCH? [ ] Yes [ ] No [X]   [ ] CUFFS   [ ] NO CUFFS

FOR IRS USE ONLY

Present Address of Addressee (must be filled out by Addressor or legal Guardian of Aforementioned (unless greater than Line B above)
The RICHMOND News Leader

City, Town, Post Office, SHOE SIZE (NO 12¼)

IS YOUR ADDRESS GREATER THAN LINE 41? [ ] No   IF YES, WHY? [ ] YES   OCC-U-PATION [ ] YOURS [ ] SPOUSE

YOU ARE Here [ ] YES [ ] NO

REQUESTED BY DEPARTMENT OF AGRICULTURE.

A. HOW MANY TALKING CHICKENS DO YOU OWN? 0.
B. NAMES   C DO ANY OF THEM PLAY THE OBOE? [ ] yes [ ] no.

DO YOU LIVE WITHIN 2 MILES OF A DECENT PIZZA PLACE? [ ] yes [ ] No [ ] EXTRA CHEESE

D. Have you Rotated your Tires Lately? [ ] yes [ ] No

IF NO, FILE IRS Tire Rotation Schedule L

E. Yes? [ ] NO
F. NO? [ ] YES

Filing Status

1 [ ] Single   [ ] Double   [ ] Sacrifice Fly

2 [ ] Married Filing Singly Joint return (even IF SPOUSE IS MARRIED SEPARATELY)

3 [ ] Joint married singly separate spouse (but FILING DOUBLE JOINTED)

4 [ ] Head of Household filing separate but joint return (if UNMARRIED BUT JOINTLY SINGLE)

5 [ ] Head of joint filing single file spouse's Separately.

6 [ ] Widow(er) with separate dependent filing Out of joint return singly

Exemptions

41 a REGULAR? [ ] yourself? [ ] Spouse [ ]

b Names of Dependent children who lived with you _____ Why? _____

c Just First names, Dummy . . . .

4 Do you weigh more than last year's tax form?

e Number of Parakeets subtracted from Gross Rotated Income (PLUS LINE 27 — UNLESS GREATER THAN TWELVE MILES) . . . . .

f How many inches in a liter? _____

7 a Total Confusion (add lines 6e AND f g; fold in eggs, beat until firm) . . .

ENTER NUMBER OF BOXES CHECKED ▶

CHECK NUMBER OF BOXES ENTERED ▶

ENTER NUMBER OF CHECKED BOXERS ▶

DO NOTHING Here ▶

8 Presidential Election Campaign Fund . . ▶ DO YOU WISH TO DESIGNATE $1 OF YOUR TAXES TO THIS WORTHY CAUSE? . . . .
WHAT ABOUT THE LITTLE LADY? . . . .

[ ] YES [ ] NO   ISN'T THIS A DUMB LAW? [ ] Yes [ ] No   NOTE: IF YOU CHECKED Yes WE WILL COME AND STEAL ALL YOUR HUBCAPS

9 Wages, Salaries, Tips, Extortion ◄ ATTACH W2 FORMS TO YOUR FOREHEAD ▶ WITH HEAVY DUTY STAPLE GUN . . . . 9.

10 Remunerations . . . [IF LESS THAN GROSS REIMBURSEMENTS, THEN FILE SCHEDULE Q (See Page 14 of "Joy of Cooking")] 10.

11 Gross Influx . . . . 11.

12 Money you made . . [IF $400 OR LESS, MORE OR LESS, LIST SCHEDULE B WITHOUT NOT FILLING IN PART II AND R2. BUT MORE THAN LINE 8] 12

13 What about all that cash you stashed in that jar under the garage?

14 SUBTRACT 13 FROM 14 . . .
15 (THE ANSWER TO 14 IS . . . 1)

Think of a number between 1 and 10

● HOW WOULD YOU LIKE A GOOD SOCK IN THE FACE, FELLA? [ ] yes [ ] No
● IF LINE 15 IS BIGGER THAN A BREADBOX OR MORE, GO TO LINE 43 TO FIGURE TAX

TAX RATE SCHEDULE X, Y, OR 12 [ ] See Page 7 of INSTRUCTIONS CHECK HERE ▶

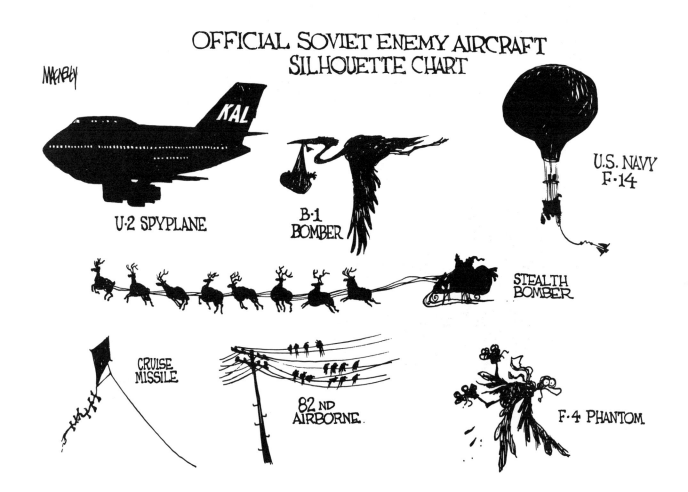

OFFICIAL SOVIET ENEMY AIRCRAFT
SILHOUETTE CHART

MACNELLY

KAL

U·2 SPYPLANE

B·1 BOMBER

U.S. NAVY F·14

STEALTH BOMBER

CRUISE MISSILE

82 ND AIRBORNE.

F·4 PHANTOM

JUST WHEN YOU THOUGHT IT WAS SAFE TO GO BACK IN THE WATER...

HEROES OF SOVIET AGRICULTURE

94 The Gang of Eight

Jeff MacNelly 95

MARLETTE

Doug Marlette

My grandfather was at various times a cotton farmer, a mill worker, a surveyor and a deputy sheriff in a rural South ravaged by the depression. He, with my grandmother, who was once bayoneted by a National Guardsman while picketing during a mill strike, sired eleven children some of whom survived hardship and disease into adulthood.

He voted for Franklin D. Roosevelt four times "...and if he was runnin' today I'd vote for him again!"

"Why is that, Granddaddy?" I asked.

"'Cause he was the only president we ever had who cared anything about the poor man." As my eyes were dewing up with populist sentimentality he added, "'Course his only mistake was he shoulda' let Hitler kill them Jews!"

This tragic counterpoint in Southern populism—the identification with the common man and contradictorily the ugly racism—was a dissonant tune played long and loudly in my family. The peculiar Southern history of invasion, defeat, humiliation, poverty and deprivation—an experience perhaps more similar to that of most of the rest of the planet than the United States as whole—is part of my inheritance.

Perhaps the vividness of the contradictions and ironies in the culture in which I grew up brought forth the satirist's rage and my impulse to "picture" those inconsistencies.

There were no artists in my family to encourage me to draw funny pictures for a living. But at age five I memorized how to draw Mickey Mouse, Donald Duck and Popeye from the comics and faithfully reproduced them for my first-grade classmates. They rewarded me with marbles and desserts. Nothing could have been more encouraging.

My interest in political cartooning was galvanized as my turbulent adolescence coincided with the unrest during the sixties. As the Vietnam War and civil rights movement was raising my political consciousness, a new, funnier, more graphically arresting style of political cartoons was rejuvenating the profession. Raised on TV, movies, comic books and *Mad* magazine this fresh new style captured my imagination. Political cartoons looked like *Mad!* I was hooked. The values I learned in Sunday school at Magnolia Street Baptist Church in Laurel, Mississippi, and in eighth grade civics classes at D. U. Maddox Junior High seem to influence my work to this day.

The kinds of cartoons I enjoy and take delight in doing are simple, direct, biting, funny and make a point. If I can come up with a drawing that touches all those bases then I am pleased. If, on top of that, I realize that nobody else would likely have done it that way, that it's got my own fingerprint on it, I'm ecstatic.

"THE COLOREDS ARE COMING! THE COLOREDS ARE COMING!"

"IF YOU HAVE TO ASK HOW MUCH, YOU CAN'T AFFORD ONE!"

★ Reagan Appointees ★

SECRETARY OF SHEEP

SECRETARY OF CHICKENS

SECRETARY OF MICE

HUMAN RIGHTS

Doug Marlette 109

" HEY, **WIMP**!....WHATCHA GOT IN THE LUNCH PAIL ?"

Doug Marlette   111

" GIVE ME YOUR RICH, YOUR FAMOUS, YOUR NOBEL LAUREATES, YOUR RUSSIAN POETS AND POLISH EMISSARIES, YOUR RESPECTABLE WHITE ANTI-SOVIETS YEARNING TO BREATHE FREE...... "

"DON'T BLAME ME—YOU'RE THE ONE WHO INSISTED ON A FROZEN EMBRYO!..."

" I SEE NO EVIDENCE OF HUNGRY CHILDREN IN AMERICA! "

"SORRY—I'VE DEPROGRAMMED MOONIES AND I'VE DEPROGRAMMED HARE KRISHNAS, BUT THERE'S NOTHING I CAN DO WITH 'YOUTH FOR REAGAN'!"

"FORTY MORE YEARS!...FORTY MORE YEARS!"

Mike Peters

Editorial cartooning is one of those great "well-kept secrets." In what other job can you spout off about injustices, insult the president, have fun and get paid all at the same time? There are people in public parks who spout their beliefs and get arrested for vagrancy. Many editorial cartoonists were the class clowns, wiseacres or campus radicals. But we also liked to draw and enjoyed irregular hours.

Luckily, I didn't take my high school counselor's advice. The only vocations he could see for me were mechanical drawing and cheerleading. I was no student and got in trouble continually for drawing critical cartoons about the principal. Recently, I was invited back to my high school to make a speech. The irony, of course, is that I am a success because I'm still doing the same thing I did then. What I have learned from all this is that to be a success you have to do what you enjoy, and success must naturally follow.

Before I went back for the speech, I decided to refresh my memory by looking over my old yearbook. Of course, it was full of my doodles and drawings. (I even signed the drawings I did on the men's-room wall.) What caught my eye was the note from my English teacher who put me in the "Vegetable Garden" in his class. His advice, not unlike the counselor was to "Shape up! After all, Mr. Peters, you can't draw cartoons all your life!"

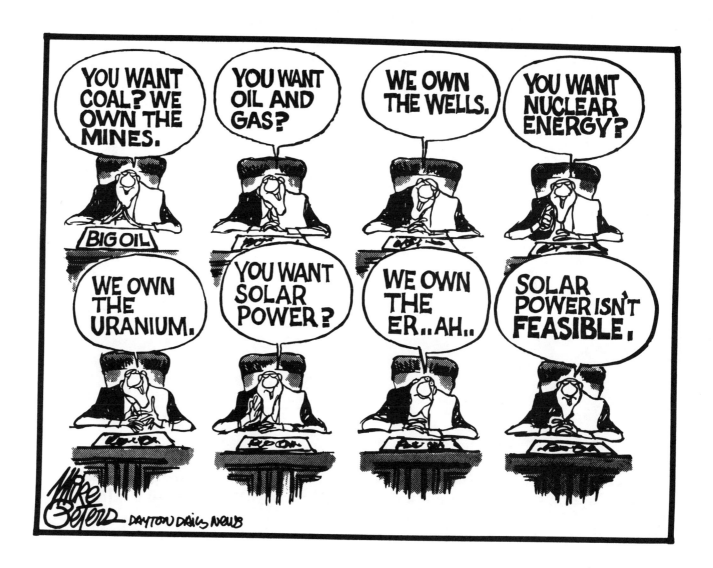

REMEMBER THE GOOD OLD DAYS WHEN WE ONLY HAD TO SMOKE A FEW CIGARETTES AND EAT SACCHARIN?

WE'VE GOT TO DEPROGRAM JUNIOR—HE'S RUN OFF AND JOINED THE PRESBYTERIANS...

MISS JONES, THIS IS SECRETARIES' WEEK... SEND YOURSELF
SOME FLOWERS WITH A NICE LITTLE NOTE...

THAT'S ODD...THEY'RE COOKED ALREADY...

HE'S GROWN A FOOT SINCE I SAW HIM LAST....

OH, ABE... STOP WORRYING ABOUT THAT NRA LOBBY GROUP AND COME TO THE THEATER WITH ME...

MISS JONES, IT'S MARGARET THATCHER'S BIRTHDAY...SEND HER SOME MARINES WITH A NICE LITTLE NOTE...

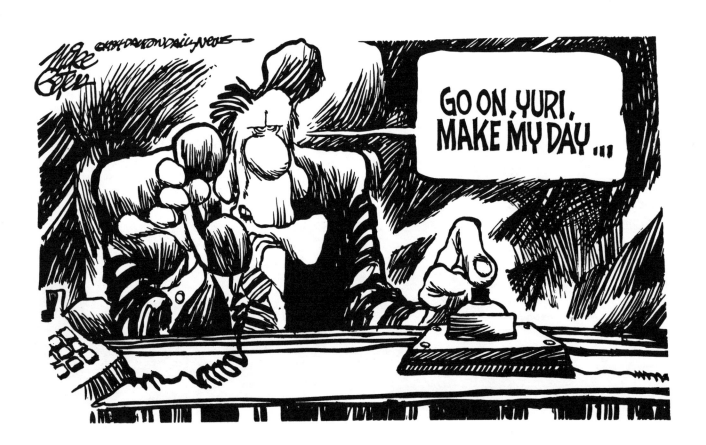

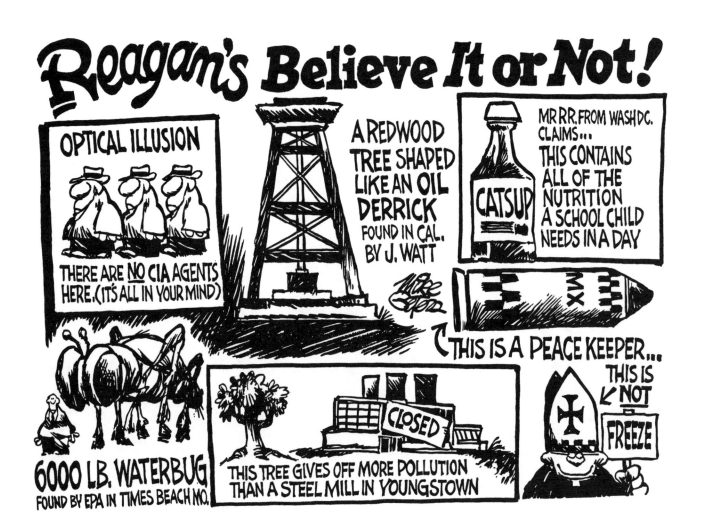

Paul Szep

I'm really a failed hockey player. I grew up in Canada and wanted very much to play in the National Hockey League. I did actually play. At the time each professional team owned certain areas, and I was under the Detroit Red Wings. In those years, Detroit had very good teams, and my prospects for making the parent club were not great. Cartooning is the other thing I did fairly well. I always thought that if I could not make it into the NHL, then I would be a cartoonist.

I actually started doing sports cartoons, combining my two loves in a sense, for the Hamilton *Spectator* when I was in high school. That was my introduction to the newspaper business, and in doing the sports cartoons, I was introduced to the political cartoons. Hamilton did not offer an intense and heavy political atmosphere—like some of my contemporaries had when they were starting out—but it did provide a nice outlet for my kind of satire. I came to view my work as primarily satire using a visual format.

I specialized in illustration for four years at the Ontario College of Art. After graduation, I freelanced as an illustrator, and then I was hired by the *Financial Post* to do cartoons and illustrations. The next thing I knew I received an invitation to come down to Boston and try out for this job at the *Globe*. They'd been looking for a political cartoonist for three or four years. The bond with the *Globe* worked instantly; it was just a good marriage from the beginning.

I am a very political individual, and I think this is reflected in my work. Some people, a lot of people in the profession, do gag cartoons, but I always try to do cartoons that make a political comment. However, I do think today that there's a difference in the kind of comment that's effective, and I think you have to use humor much more than in the past. But I like to think of cartooning as satire, biting humor. It is very hard for me to do something trite, yet I know the American public probably appreciates that kind of humor more than they do the heavier handed type.

Getting the ideas for the cartoons is definitely the hardest part of the process. Getting up every morning and knowing that you have to make a comment, that you have to come up with something. I probably go through four or five newspapers every day. You're always looking for something, trying to think of something, that you can comment on. You're always looking for some basic inequity. You're always looking for some asshole in politics who's out there flogging himself. There's always a plethora of subjects. It's just a case of trying to sit down and decide which you can make work best; what subject matter will work the best. I think cartoonists should be like burrs under the saddle of some egomaniac, kind of gnawing away every day. I think the public likes cartoons because it gives them a vicarious pleasure that they normally can't get in any other way. It must be very frustrating never to have that kind of outlet. Having said that, I must say I really enjoy what I'm doing. I take great pleasure in having that release every day.

I've always said that I don't know whether it's an advantage or a prerequisite, but I think a cartoonist should be able to ride the elevator of life. You should be able to get off at the bottom floor, the top floor and at all the middle floors; you should be able to wander around there and make observations. To watch people of all walks of life and of all socio-economic levels is essential. It's also good to have a sense of humor and to realize that really you are only a cartoonist. I think you should never forget that. You have a particular role to perform—and in a way, it is performed—but in the overall scheme of things, it is a very limited role.

'A Senator Fulbright to See You, Sire. Seems He Can't
Reconcile Himself to Your Infallibility.'

"I've decided not to tell you about the alleged shipwreck."

"Snow White's still at large."

"I'll be Jack Kennedy . . . who do you want to be?"

Queen Elizabeth visits the US in honor of the Bicentennial.

Paul Szep 155

THE NIXON INTERVIEW . . . WARTS AND ALL

"I tried to beat them for 70 bucks . . . how about you?"

"Accursed be he that first invented war"

A
POLITICIAN
SHOULD
BE
TRUSTWORTHY
LOYAL
HELPFUL
FRIENDLY
COURTEOUS
KIND
OBEDIENT
CHEERFUL
THRIFTY
BRAVE
CLEAN
REVERENT

IRANIANS CLAIM CAPABILITY TO MAKE THEIR OWN CHEMICAL ARMS

British Ace

Nixon still defends Vietnam on 10th anniversary of prisoner-of-war release.

"SPEAK SOFTLY AND CARRY A BIG SHTIK ... "

164   The Gang of Eight

'I've seen your movies and TV shows . . . but I just love the way you play
an American President best!'

The Great Debate, No. 1

DEMOCRATIC GOVERNORS URGE
MONDALE TO DEFINE HIS PERSONALITY BETTER

©THE BOSTON GLOBE

'Define my what?'

"Tell him, I said, 'If he doesn't pass the cream, I'll level half of Moscow' ...
Ha, Ha ... just joking"

Don Wright

Tom Wolfe was right! New-wealth professionals have heady ambitions for the arts: welded iron pseudo-shapes, colored boxes juxtaposed and glued into "spatial relationships" and foolish swaths of geometric color on canvas. They are "in," deemed legitimate, sought after and expensive. Where, I ask, do political cartoonists fit in the world of yuppie art and in the world of newspaper art?

Generally, the public is comatose these days when it comes to the study and appreciation of fine art, leaving all interpretation and judgment to the "experts." (This is, after all, the age of specialization. If you have "art," you must have experts to explain it.)

It does not stretch credibility to suggest that the cultural vacuum, witnessed by what is happening in the field of contemporary art, has already spilled over into newspapers and is affecting editorial cartoonists. And that is, principally, because people don't read anymore, critically or otherwise. It doesn't take a Marshall McLuhan devotee to understand the consequences, does it? If reading is no longer part of the national psyche, will newspapers continue to survive?

Some editors have tried to lure readers back with slapdash colored boxes or garish and unwieldly teases and charts thrown onto pages like so much random paint splatter. We call this affliction "graphics." It peaked with the introduction of the trendy, national publication, *USA Today,* dedicated to the proposition that most readers have suppressed any residual, natural inclination to read for detail. If more editors seek this level and continue to write down to it, reportorial standards will decrease sharply and with them the bite and inquisitiveness needed to keep readers informed.

If you believe the editorial page is the last bastion of logic, detail and persuasion and is immune from this onslaught of superficiality, consider editorial cartoons and editorial cartoonists. In most cases, they splash happily about in this "Great Tide of Tasteless Art," generally with the approval and encouragement of editors, producing reams of uninspired, no, worse, "funny" little figures acting out some half-baked, often-obscure caption. All this is done in the true belief that mediocrity and humor will not offend and is what the public demands. Gone is the pamphleteering spirit of our revolutionary ancestors, to whom debate and political controversy were noble persuasions.

If fine artists, of whatever immediate reputation, are the traditionally-accepted chroniclers of history, what then, are we political cartoonists? Are we really artists or simply an occassionally clever, but passionless, filler in a nervous newspaper?

Until these questions are answered, the general state of editorial cartoon art may well be that it is not art at all.

BURGER COURT

CONSTITUT

UNITED STAT

..AND SO GOD CREATED MOSS.

 ..WHICH WASHED ASHORE, MIXED WITH OXYGEN AND BECAME LICHEN.

 IN 400,000 YEARS LICHENS GREW EYES.

 ..AND A LITTLE BODY AND BECAME A WORM.

 4.2 MILLION YEARS LATER IT HAD GROWN LEGS AND ARMS WITH WHICH IT LEARNED TO HANDLE IMPLEMENTS.

WRIGHT ©1981 MIAMI NEWS

 TIME PASSED. LIMBS GREW LONGER AND MORE DEXTEROUS AND THE HEAD CHANGED SHAPE. THE LICHENWORM LOOKED LIKE THIS:

 AND IT WAS CALLED MAN AND MAN MONKEYED AROUND WITH ALL KINDS OF THINGS. ..FOR USE AGAINST THE GODLESS!

 ..AND SO GOD CREATED MOSS.

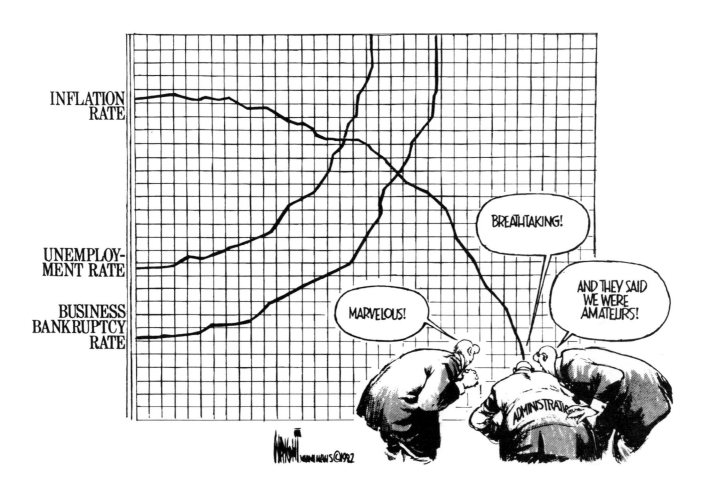

In this season, dedicated to the spirit of love and the uplifting of all humankind, we bring you Christmas greetings from...

...Florida.

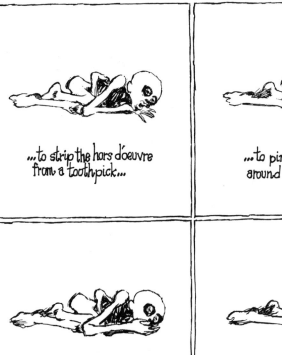

In the time it takes...

...to strip the hors d'oeuvre from a toothpick...

...to pinch the fat around your waist...

...to hear a politician extol the good life...

...to count the jowls on religious hucksters...

...another child will starve to death in Ethiopia.

Don Wright 191

192   The Gang of Eight

PT261 901